IVANHOE

NOTES

ncluding
- *Introduction*
- *Life and Background*
- *List of Characters*
- *Brief Synopsis*
- *Summaries and Commentaries*
- *Character Sketches*
- *Critical Notes*
- *Glossary*
- *Examination and Review Questions*
- *Selected Bibliography*

P9-DGT-906

y
Norma Ostrander, M.A.
University of Nebraska

REVISED EDITION

INCORPORATED

LINCOLN, NEBRASKA 68501

$2.93 BEL 387 3

Editor

Gary Carey, M.A.
University of Colorado

Consulting Editor

James L. Roberts, Ph.D.
Department of English
University of Nebraska

REVISED EDITION
ISBN 0-8220-0663-4
© Copyright 1967, 1962
by
C. K. Hillegass

All Rights Reserved
Printed in U.S.A

Cliffs Notes, Inc.   Lincoln, Nebraska

CONTENTS

Ivanhoe

INTRODUCTION

The title of Sir Walter Scott's most popular and best-known novel is derived from an old rhyme which records the names of three manors forfeited by a nobleman for striking the Black Prince with his tennis racket. "Tring, Wing, and Ivanhoe" were the three estates. Scott chose "Ivanhoe" for two reasons: it has an ancient English sound and it gives no indication of the subject matter of the story.

The first paragraph of *Ivanhoe* sets the stage for the whole.

In that pleasant district of merry England which is watered by the river Don, there extended in ancient times a large forest, covering the greater part of the beautiful hills and valleys which lie between Sheffield and the pleasant town of Doncaster.... Here haunted of yore the fabulous Dragon of Wantley; here were fought many of the most desperate battles of the Civil Wars of the Roses; and here also flourished in ancient times those bands of gallant outlaws, whose deeds have been rendered so popular in English song.

The action all takes place in the environs of York, Lincoln, and Sheffield, mostly in the rural areas surrounding these ancient towns. Scott in vivid terms paints the natural beauty of England much as it is today, although there were no hedgerows in the twelfth century and although many Norman castles, gaping ruins now, were then in the splendor of their prime. The forests were there, however, and the glades and streams. These had changed little with the centuries.

LIFE OF SCOTT

Walter Scott was born in Edinburgh, Scotland, August 15, 1771. His father was a farmer and his mother, Anne Rutherford, was the daughter of Dr. John Rutherford, who was one of the founders of the medical school of Edinburgh. Mrs. Scott was fond of poetry and anecdotes and it was from her that Walter received inspiration.

Walter was one of ten children. The other children's only claim to fame was that they had, "good health and untameable spirits." In contrast, Walter was afflicted at twenty-one months with something which a biographer describes as, "a paralytic affection, superinduced, or at least aggravated by scrofulous habit of body." It is sufficient to say that it made him lame and doubtless pushed him into more academic pursuits.

He spent much time with his grandparents, but it was "Aunt Jenny" who took a special interest in him and influenced him to write. His visits to an uncle, Dr. Rutherford, professor of botany at the University of Edinburgh, brought him into contact with scholarly people.

His parents were very religious and imposed strict piety upon all their children. Walter was never very deeply affected religiously, however. His works, which contain much about the church, seek neither to elevate nor to censure it, but rather to depict it, for it was history and not philosophy that interested him most.

His first novel, *Waverly,* was published anonymously. Although Scott probably never intended that "Laurence Templeton" should be taken as a real person, he was attempting to remain in anonymity by the use of the name. His publishers persuaded him to allow further novels to be designated as "by the author of *Waverly,*" and for this reason some of his novels were called the "Waverly Novels." Although he published biographies of Swift and Dryden and some history, as well as poems and novels, his chief claim to distinction is his contribution to Romanticism and the historical novel.

He suffered from many physical ailments, one particularly serious one in adolescence, which made him, in his own words, "a glutton of books." Scott became seriously ill before *Ivanhoe* was finished and dictated much of it from his sickbed.

His popularity, both socially and as a writer, was almost unparalleled. He was married in 1797 to Margaret Charlotte Carpenter, who bore him three sons and two daughters. Scott received his title and baronetcy from King George IV in the spring of 1820. He died, Sir Walter Scott, in 1832.

BACKGROUND FOR *IVANHOE*

Chivalry was the code of conduct that governed the knights and noblemen of the Middle Ages. Tennyson in *Gareth and Lynette* expressed its ideals in the words: "Follow the deer? Follow the Christ, the King, Live pure, speak true, right wrong, follow the King—Else, wherefore born?" Respect for women, truth, honor, and courage were also expected. Chaucer's knight loved "chivalrye, trouthe and honour, fredom and courteisye."

The Crusades were organized to drive the Turkish invaders out of the Holy Land, particularly Bethlehem, birthplace of Christ, and Jerusalem, where he was crucified. Churchmen, princes, knights, and noblemen united in this attempt, some going because of religious zeal and others because of the opportunity to travel. There were seven Crusades in all, lasting from 1096 to 1291. All were eventually unsuccessful, and the Moslem conquerors were at last left in possession of the holy shrines.

The feudal system embraced all strata of society in the Middle Ages. Each nobleman, or overlord, divided his land among lesser nobles, or gentlemen, who became his vassals. These grants of land were called fiefs. In return for his lord's protection, the vassal paid certain rents and pledged himself to fight for his liege. Serfs, who were bound to the land, constituted the lowest class. A few franklins, or freeholders, held their lands independently.

Knighthood was the aspiration of every highborn youth, and most of his education was pointed in that direction, unless he was preparing to enter the church. At seven he became a page in the household of a knight or a nobleman. At fourteen he was a squire, helping his lord with horse and armor and caring for his protector if wounded or killed. Training for knighthood included practice in the use of lance, sword, battleaxe, and the wearing of armor, but most knights could neither read nor write. Such learning was reserved for churchmen.

At twenty-one the young squire took the vows of knighthood and received armor, spurs, and sword in a solemn ceremony. Last of all he received his war horse. Now he was ready for adventure in the jousts or in battle.

Knights Templars were a special order of knights whose duty was to guard the Holy Sepulchre. In addition to the vows of knighthood, they were bound not to marry. They also were taught to read and write. Their chief establishment in England was in the area of London still called the Temple.

The Norman Conquest occurred in 1066 when William of Normandy invaded southern England and won a decisive victory over the Saxon Harold at Battle, a few miles from Hastings. William vowed that if he were successful he would build an abbey on the spot where Harold fell. Battle Abbey, not the original one, but a superb medieval structure of stone, is a tourist attraction today. William the Conqueror and his successors found it hard, however, to enforce Norman rule on the conquered Saxons, and not until the fourteenth century did the intermixture of the two peoples become complete. The time of *Ivanhoe* is approximately a century after the Norman Conquest.

The Plantagenet kings, who ruled England from 1216 to 1399, were so-called because the father of Henry II, a Frenchman, wore a sprig of yellow broom flower in his helmet. This bright-hued flower still grows wild along the roadside in southern France. Richard I was the second of the Plantagenet kings (*plante gênet*).

Robin Hood, the popular hero of song and story, probably lived in the twelfth century and with his band of outlaws furnished excitement in Sherwood Forest. As Locksley in *Ivanhoe*, he demonstrates his unmatchable skill with bow and arrow. Traditionally he robbed the rich to give to the poor. With his name were associated those of his chief followers: Little John, Friar Tuck, Allan-a-Dale, and Maid Marian, fair "as ivory bone."

The tournaments were to the Middle Ages what baseball and football games and other athletic events are to modern spectators. Usually called by invitation of a prince or a nobleman, they were practice sessions for war. Knights showed their prowess and developed their skill. The tournament at Ashby-de-la-Zouche actually occurred, Scott using it as part of his historic background.

LIST OF CHARACTERS

Cedric
> Saxon thane; called by the Normans a franklin.

Wilfred of Ivanhoe
> Son of Cedric; follower of King Richard.

Rowena
> Ward of Cedric; descendant of King Alfred.

Athelstane
> Cedric's choice of a husband for Rowena; descendant of noble Saxon line.

Isaac
> Jewish moneylender of York.

Rebecca
> Isaac's daughter; skilled in the art of healing.

Richard Plantagenet
> King Richard of England; called the Lion-Hearted king. He was made captive by the Duke of Austria on his way back to England from a Crusade.

John Plantagenet
> Brother of Richard who occupied throne during King Richard's absence.

Waldemar Fitzurse
> Adviser to Prince John.

Maurice de Bracy
> Knight attached to Prince John's retinue.

Philip Malvoisin

Norman in league with Prince John.

Albert Malvoisin

Preceptor at Templestowe.

Front de Boeuf

Norman lord to whom Prince John had given the fief of Ivanhoe.

Prior Aymer of Jorvaulx

Cisterian monk of the Abbey of Jorvaulx.

Brian de Bois-Guilbert

Knight of the Order of Knights Templar recently returned from Crusades.

Lucas Beaumanoir

Grand Master of the Knights Templar.

Locksley (Robin Hood)

Leader of the band of forest outlaws.

Friar Tuck (Clerk of Copmanhurst)

Hedge Priest of the outlaw band.

Allan-a-Dale

Minstrel member of outlaws.

Ulrica (Urfried)

Crone in the castle of Torquilstone; daughter of Torquil Wolfganger, friend of Cedric's father.

Wamba

Jester bondsman of Cedric.

Gurth

Swineherd for Cedric.

Edith

Athelstane's mother.

Elgitha

Rowena's maid.

Nathan Ben Israel

Hebrew Rabbi, adviser to Isaac.

Oswald

Cedric's cupbearer.

Higg, Son of Snell

Peasant witness at Rebecca's trial.

Conrade de Mont-Fitchet

Preceptor of Templestowe.

BRIEF SYNOPSIS

Four generations and approximately one hundred years had passed since the decisive Battle of Hastings in 1066. Richard the Lion-Hearted (1157-1199), now King of England, on returning from the Crusades, was made prisoner of the Duke of Austria, abetted by the machinations of Richard's brother, Prince John. Prince John hoped, by the help of his Norman confederates, to seize the throne.

Wilfred of Ivanhoe, son of Cedric, had been disinherited by his father for two reasons: because of his allegiance to Richard, the exiled King of England, and because of his romantic interest in Rowena, ward of Cedric, whom Cedric intended as bride to Athelstane, a descendant of Saxon royalty.

In the guise of the Disinherited Knight, Ivanhoe wins the tournament at Ashby-de-la-Zouche with the aid of the Black Knight and crowns Rowena his Queen of Beauty and Love. He suffers severe wounds in the contest and is ministered to by Rebecca, daughter of the Jewish moneylender, Isaac of York.

On the way home from the tournament the Saxon party, together with the Jews and the wounded Ivanhoe, are captured by De Bracy, who fancies Rowena as his wife. They are taken to the castle of Front-de-Boeuf and imprisoned there. The Black Knight, Locksley and his band, Cedric, and others attack the castle and, with the help of Ulrica, an old Saxon hag, succeed in freeing the prisoners. Brian de Bois-Guilbert, Knight Templar, escapes to Templestowe, taking Rebecca with him.

Rebecca, accused of sorcery, is sentenced to die as a witch. Ivanhoe champions her in a trial by combat against the unwilling Bois-Guilbert. Rebecca is set free when the Templar falls dead from his horse.

The Black Knight reveals himself as King Richard, Ivanhoe and Rowena are married, and Rebecca and her father leave England for Granada.

SUMMARIES AND COMMENTARIES

CHAPTER 1

Summary

In the opening chapter, Scott describes the setting and gives a historical account of England during the reign of Richard I.

With the captivity of King Richard, the nobles had resumed the practice of making vassals and serfs of their less powerful neighbors. The hostility of the Saxons, which began with the victory of Duke William of Normandy at the Battle of Hastings, was kept smoldering by the Norman French, who reduced many of the Saxons to servitude, and seized, or threatened to seize, their lands.

French became the official language and, although a common dialect emerged, each faction spoke the other's language as little as possible.

As Gurth, with the aid of his dog, gathers the swine, he and Wamba discuss the Norman-Saxon community. Just as they are leaving to avoid the approaching storm, they hear a party of horsemen approaching.

Commentary

Wamba and Gurth show two aspects of the bondsman. Wamba is dressed richly and lives by his wits. Gurth wears coarser garb and tends swine as a menial. Both wear the slave collar.

Several instances point up the Norman-Saxon conflict. The dog, Fangs, whose foreclaws have been clipped by the ranger of the forest in accord with the Forest Laws enacted by the ruling Normans, symbolizes by his name and description the stripping of power from the Saxons.

Wamba refers to the language: specifically, the word "swine" is of Saxon origin and used when the animals are being tended and fed, but becomes "pork," a French word, when it is ready for the table. "Alderman Ox" is a Saxon term, which becomes "beef," a French word, when it is ready for consumption.

Gurth is a second "Eumaeus." Eumaeus was the swineherd in Homer's *Odyssey* who chafed under tending the swine for the consumption of the wooers of Penelope while Odysseus was absent.

CHAPTERS 2-4

Summary

The horsemen prove to be Brian de Bois-Guilbert, the Knight Templar, and his companion Prior Aymer, worldly minded Abbot of Jorvaulx, and their attendants. Wamba misdirects them as they seek to find the home of Cedric the Saxon. Before they reach a sunken cross where the paths meet, they have a lively discussion which ends in a wager concerning the beauty and desirability of Rowena, Cedric's ward. At the foot of the cross they find a Palmer who accompanies them to Cedric's home.

Rotherwood, Cedric's home, its furnishings, the clothing, and rank of the occupants, are described in great detail. When the Templar and the Prior arrive, they are treated with hospitality The Palmer, inconspicuous by his dress, is scarcely noticed. Just as Cedric and his guests prepare to eat, Wamba and Gurth arrive, and a few minutes later Lady Rowena joins the group.

Commentary

The total picture of the medieval church is made plain as Scott describes each of her adherents. Aymer, Prior of the Abbey of Jorvaulx, "under the penthouse of his eyes" has an "epicurean twinkle." The word penthouse, in less elegant terms, bags under his eyes, suggests he is dissipated. His epicurean twinkle reveals his love of good food and drink, and a "cautious voluptuary" is one who appeases his fleshly appetites under cover of piety. His garb, while correct for his order, is decorated so that it resembles the somber dress of a "Quaker beauty" who chooses rich materials and wears them so as to show her beauty to advantage.

Brian de Bois-Guilbert represents the military aspect of the church. He is arrogant and stern, and relies upon strict discipline to maintain his superiority. He uses Norman-French, the language of the "superior classes," and he would not ask for hospitality of Cedric, but demand it.

The Palmer, although even his demeanor is a disguise, is representative of the gentler following of the cross.

The prejudice against the Moslem faith is felt in the term "Old Mahmoud," which is a derogatory name for Mahomet. The Crusades are called the "excess of blood-guiltiness" by Cedric, but his is bitterness against a disobedient son rather than criticism. He later praises them.

The furnishings of Cedric's house, though crude, suggest wealth and power and an attempt to preserve the flavor of existence before the Norman conquest. The seating arrangement shows the caste system of the feudal manor. Cedric, himself, epitomizes the unconquerable spirit of the Saxon lord.

In Chapters 2 and 3 the author uses the device of foreshadowing, giving the reader a hint of what is to come. Chapter 2 has references to Cedric's disinherited son and to the beauty, nobility, and rank of Rowena, who has not yet appeared in the story. Chapter 3 mentions a connection between Cedric's banished son and the Crusades in Palestine.

Note Cedric's reference to "William the Bastard." William the Conqueror was an illegitimate ruler, not a true son of England. Cedric defers to the French, however, either to impress or appease them, by setting out the best food and drink. He is stirred to angry reflection by the mention of "curfew," an imposition of the Normans.

Cedric's wish to protect Rowena from contact with Brian de Bois-Guilbert and his reproof at the Templar's bold stare show that he is aware of the perfidious nature of the Templars.

Vortigen was a prince who invited Hengist the Saxon to England and married his daughter, Rowena. The reference here is to the invasion of Britain by the Vikings, which parallels the invasion by the French. The Templar is being both ironic and bold.

Wamba's comment about "truces with infidels" is a general one about the lack of honor among truce-makers.

Cedric's final speech in Chapter 4, with its reference to the elements raging outside, suggests a paraphrasing of a passage from Shakespeare's *King Lear*.

CHAPTERS 5-6

The Jew, Isaac of York, is introduced in these chapters. His dealings with the Palmer herald further meetings of the two. In conversation, Cedric learns of Ivanhoe's prowess in the Crusades and the Palmer pledges a meeting between Ivanhoe and Brian de Bois-Guilbert.

By his knowledge of the language of the Saracen slaves the Palmer uncovers a plot by the Templar to rob Isaac. When the Palmer helps the Jew escape, Isaac rewards him with a loan of horse and armor for the coming tournament at Ashby-de-la-Zouche.

Commentary

The hatred for the Jew infects everyone, both Saxon and Norman, from the lords and knights to the lowest menial. Even the Palmer, who shows mercy, is not without prejudice. As he says, "it beseems not men of my character and thine to travel together longer than need be." Isaac enlists little sympathy, however, for his greed and claim to poverty are well characterized.

Note Wamba's remark about the Jew stealing a "gammon of bacon." Pork was an abomination to the Jew.

The tax imposed by the Exchequer upon the Jews was indeed heavy. It was a means of reprisal for the usury practiced by the Jewish moneylenders.

The hunting terms in this section were the highly particular words coined each year about which no French gentleman dared be ignorant. The beginning of this science is credited to Sir Tristem (Tristem and Ysolde).

The identity of Ivanhoe in the disguise of the Palmer is indicated by his intelligence, his conversation with Rowena, and his apparent power over Gurth. Gurth's change of attitude after the Palmer's words with him show that Gurth has some reason to be in awe of the Palmer and to show his obeisance.

Summary

The tournament with its colorful pavilions and the excited and varied crowds of spectators are described in vivid detail. Rebecca, beautiful daughter of Isaac, is introduced for the first time. A Norman-Saxon quarrel over the seating of Isaac and Rebecca is solved in an unexpected manner by Wamba, the Jester. Other characters introduced are Athelstane, of Saxon royalty and suitor of Rowena, and Waldemar Fitzurse, counselor to Prince John.

On the first day the Disinherited Knight overthrows four stalwart opponents, unhorses Brian de Bois-Guilbert, whom he has challenged to mortal combat, and presents the coronet to Rowena, designating her as the Queen of Beauty and Love for the second day. The victor and his queen decline the invitation to attend the banquet given by Prince John.

Commentary

Against the background of political intrigue and the miserable social conditions in England, the spectacle of the tournament stands out in vivid relief. King Richard has been absent from his realm, reputedly a prisoner of the Duke of Austria. Prince John, the crafty younger brother in league with Philip of France, has been using every available means to prolong Richard's captivity and at the same time to dispose of young Arthur, son of an older brother, Geoffrey, who is next in line for the throne.

Isaac, protected by the general law of England, and more particularly by those who owe him money, or like Prince John, are in the act of negotiating a loan, exhibits a different mien and appearance than when he was the recipient of Cedric's hospitality. Only the yeoman outlaw, who knows no law, causes him anxiety.

The knights, even those who had fought in the Crusades, have divided loyalties. The jousting sometimes becomes more bellicose because of the allegiance some orders feel for the absent king.

Scott makes a general comment about the license of royalty, not only as characteristic of Prince John, but of royalty and the highborn in general, when he writes, "such expression ['that sort of comeliness which belongs to an open nature'] is often mistaken for manly frankness, when in truth it arises from the reckless indifference of a libertine disposition, conscious of superiority of birth, of wealth . . . totally unconnected with personal merit."

Athelstane, called derisively, the "Unready," represents the apathy which people often adopt toward a change of fortune. Although Cedric is attached to a losing cause, sympathy tends to be with his active resistance.

Prince John's proposal of Rebecca as a candidate for queen, might have been effective as a show of tolerance, when, in truth, it was used only to incite the anger of the Saxons.

The names, Malvoisin (bad neighbor) and Front-de-Beouf (Ox-face) help to characterize the unpopular barons.

Whatever Scott's intention, the Spanish term, "Desdichado" for Disinherited, serves to symbolize Ivanhoe's alienation from the father who had disowned him and from the Normans from whom he was alienated by birth.

The power of Fitzurse is demonstrated by the conciliatory measures he takes to cover Prince John's lack of wisdom. His self-appointed role of adviser, while for self-advancement, often saves face for Prince John.

CHAPTERS 10-11

Summary

The Disinherited Knight, as custom dictates, is presented with the choice of the horses and armor or equivalent ransom from each of the five knights whom he has vanquished. He accepts ransom money from four of them but refuses to take anything from the squire of Bois-Guilbert on the grounds of the "mortal defiance" between them.

Gurth is sent to pay the eighty zecchins to Isaac for the use of horse and armor in the recent combat. Rebecca secretly restores the money, adding twenty zecchins for Gurth.

On the return trip, Gurth thinks of the time when he will have money to purchase his freedom. He is set upon by robbers, who surprisingly restore his money and give him safe conduct to the place of the lists.

Commentary

These intermediary chapters serve to show the character of the Jewess, whose wisdom overshadows her father's lamentations and avarice. Her observation that "We are like the herb which flourisheth most when it is most trampled upon" expresses a common notion of the benefits of persecution.

That they are no ordinary thieves who attack Gurth is shown by their unusual clemency. These are thieves who have become what they are in protest and among whom there is honor.

Note the allusion to necromancy and cabal, which Gurth fears, as a portent of Rebecca's fate.

Sir Walter Scott injects himself into the story (authorial intrusion) as when in Chapter 11 he says "we" must do in prose what we can to honor the quarter-staff battle between Gurth and the miller. The quarter-staff battle is part of the legend surrounding Robin Hood and his gang.

CHAPTER 12

Summary

The excitement on the second day of the tournament reaches a climax as the Disinherited Knight is assaulted at the same time by Athelstane, Front-de-Boeuf, and Brian de Bois-Guilbert. With the aid of the Black Sluggard he succeeds in overthrowing Athelstane and Front-de-Boeuf. The Templar's horse goes down under the charge of the Disinherited Knight and "Desdichado" becomes the victor for the second time. The Black Sluggard retires when the odds are evened, and he disappears when the Disinherited Knight is victorious.

When Rowena crowns the victor, his head is bared and his identity as Ivanhoe is revealed. His wound is so severe, however, that he faints at Rowena's feet.

Commentary

This chapter appeals primarily to the senses of sight and sound. The sense of action is conveyed as the sights and sounds of battle would assail the spectator rather than as the participant would feel and react.

The chant of the crowd "Death is better than defeat!" is characteristic of the code of chivalry. The courage to dare, even in the face of overwhelming odds, was the only courage worth having. Other cries of the heralds exemplify the medieval code of honor.

Disguise, however thin, was a device Scott used over and over to create suspense and add drama to the narrative. Even though the reader isn't fooled for long, the dramatic climax of revelation is good entertainment.

There is irony as Scott describes the tournament (its fatalities and injuries), then gives its name — "The Gentle and Joyous Passage of Arms of Ashby."

CHAPTERS 13-15

Summary

With the identity of Ivanhoe revealed, there is much speculation as to whether Front-de-Boeuf will be forced to relinquish the castle he now occupies, previously assigned by Richard to Ivanhoe. Prince John, whose plan for wedding Rowena to De Bracy is in the making, is quite agitated when he receives a billet saying, "Take heed to yourself, for the Devil is unchained."

Even though the main event of the day is over, lesser contests are still to come, among them the archery contest in which Locksley easily defeats Hubert.

At the royal banquet that evening, Cedric offends Prince John by drinking to the health of Richard the Lion-Hearted.

De Bracy, fascinated with the idea of wedding Rowena, dons yeoman's clothes and plans to abduct the Saxon party as they return home from the tournament. Fitzurse, who has been busy recouping the loyalty of Prince John's wavering subjects, looks upon De Bracy's folly with disfavor.

Commentary

The insecurity of Prince John is revealed by his agitation over the message. ("The devil is unchained" refers, of course, to the escape of Richard the Lion-Hearted from captivity.) In contrast to Prince John's panic, Fitzurse coolly plans a counteraction. Prince John's lack of wisdom is evident when in the next chapter he seeks to curry favor by inviting the Saxon notables to the banquet, and then subjecting them to ridicule, thus defeating his own purpose. His weaknesses are most apparent to those whose fortunes rest with his, particularly Fitzurse and De Bracy, who covet high positions in the event Prince John becomes King of England.

Scott introduces a good deal of irony by exposing the bad manners of the Normans and the gluttonous ones of the Saxons. He continues the expose of the medieval church by recounting the impious antics of the Prior.

The archery contest is a bit more than a pleasant interlude. It serves to introduce the character and skill of Locksley, whom the reader will recognize as Robin Hood, and to show the loyalty of many kinds of people to the dispossessed king.

Fitzurse demonstrates great ingenuity as he cajoles, threatens, or bribes the wavering followers of Prince John back into the fold of the arrogant prince.

The drinking of a health to Richard by Cedric is symbolic of the changing attitude of the Saxon from mass hatred for the Normans to consideration for the worth of the individual.

CHAPTERS 16-17

Summary

The Black Knight, who had disappeared before his identity was questioned too much, reappears in these chapters wandering in the forest. He comes upon the hermitage of the Clerk of Copmanhurst, whom the reader will recognize as the curtal friar of Fountain's Abbey, Friar Tuck of Robin Hood's band. When a mutual trust is established, the Friar and the Black Knight drink and sing together in lusty conviviality.

Commentary

Friar Tuck, who says facetiously that he bolts his door against robbers, is a type of disreputable "holy man" who traveled with men of notorious character. Though pretending to be saintly, he is, in reality, a poacher, a heavy drinker, a lover of good food and drink, and unschooled. His status with the church was that of an "unfrocked priest," and Scott, who borrowed the incidents involving the Friar from an old romance, probably did not intend his lack of piety to be a serious indictment of the church.

The words of the songs which the Black Knight and the Friar sing show a kind of "spoof" on the sanctity of each partaker's vocation—knighthood and the church.

CHAPTERS 18-21

Summary

When Cedric is satisfied that Ivanhoe is in good hands, he and his party start home. Gurth is recognized by Oswald and bound as a captive for having attended Ivanhoe. During the ride he slips his bonds and escapes, renouncing his service to Cedric. The superstitious Saxons are frightened by the howling of Fangs, sure that it is a sign of impending evil.

As they journey through the wood, they encounter Isaac and Rebecca with a sick man on a horse-drawn litter. Rebecca implores Rowena for protection and the request is granted.

In the assumed character of yeoman outlaws, De Bracy and his band swoop down upon the travelers and take them all prisoners except Wamba, who escapes. Wamba meets Locksley, who offers to help them. Locksley gathers his band and sends them on various errands. He, Wamba, and Gurth, whom Wamba finds in the woods, go to the chapel, where they find the Friar and the Black Knight in hilarious camaraderie. Both pledge assistance to the prisoners, who have been taken to Torquilstone, the castle of Front-de-Boeuf, and have been confined in different rooms in the building.

Commentary

Cedric, desiring to rebuild a Saxon empire through the lineage of Rowena and Athelstane, chooses to overlook the total unfitness of Athelstane for the position of ruler. Athelstane's main interest is food and drink.

By including the incident of the dog's howling, Scott is portraying the superstitious nature of many Saxons of that time.

Locksley's eagerness to aid Wamba and Gurth may be motivated as much by a desire to punish those who dare to impersonate his band as by concern for the prisoners. As he says, "our honour is concerned to punish them, and we will find a means to do so."

Knighthood, whose very foundations were honor, has a poor example in Brian de Bois-Guilbert. De Bracy shows his knowledge of this lack as the Templar replies to De Bracy's distrust in regard to Rowena, "Psha, what hast thou to fear? Thou knowest the vows of our order." "Right well," says De Bracy, "and also how well they are kept."

Scott, who is at his best with the lower classes, makes Wamba a "wise fool." For example, he says, "I have heard men talk of the blessings of freedom, but I wish any wise man would teach me what use to make of it now that I have it." Gurth, too, finds freedom burdensome when his master is taken captive. He says, more sagaciously than usual, in answer to Wamba's reference to Gurth's having declared he will never return to Cedric's service, "That was but while he was fortunate."

CHAPTERS 22-23

Summary

Isaac of York is thrown into the dungeon-vault of the castle and threatened with slow torture by fire unless he delivers to Front-de-Beouf a thousand pounds of silver. The Jew asks that his daughter be sent to York under safe conduct to procure the money, only to learn that she has been made the special property of Brian de Bois-Guilbert. The sound of the bugle breaks off the preparations for the torture.

In another part of the castle, Lady Rowena is approached by De Bracy with a proposal of marriage. She learns for the first time that the wounded Ivanhoe is also a prisoner in the castle and that if she refuses De Bracy, Wilfred and Cedric will be the price of her refusal. She uses her only weapon, tears, and both she and De Bracy are relieved by the bugle summons.

Commentary

Scott cites actual cases of extreme cruelty practiced in the eleventh and twelfth centuries to establish authenticity for the torture intended for Isaac. Up to this point either obsequious or avaricious, Isaac shows a better side to his nature. His love for his daughter is genuine, for she is the one thing more precious to him than money.

The character of the Lady Rowena is an example of the flower of womanhood. She is fair, chaste, and noble. Even the sensual

De Bracy falters at her tears. While Front-de-Boeuf's one-dimensional cruelty is exhibited in the scene with Isaac, De Bracy's more believable character is demonstrated in the scene with Rowena. He greatly desires to make Rowena his, but is moved and wavers at the evidence of her agony.

The sound of the bugle, whether deliberately or unintentionally on Scott's part, is the symbol of reprieve for the captives and judgment on the captors. It is, to be sure, ironical, since it is sounded by a thief.

CHAPTERS 24-27

Summary

Rebecca, like Rowena, is being wooed by a man she dislikes, Brian de Bois-Guilbert. Unlike De Bracy, however he does not propose marriage. When she repulses his advances, threatening to jump from the tower, he is moved to admiration. When the trumpet sounds, he, too, is forced to heed its summons.

A letter from the Black Knight and Locksley, bearing the signatures of Gurth and Wamba, demands the release of the imprisoned party. In reply to the missive Front-de-Beouf asks that a man of religion be sent to hear the confessions of the doomed captives. Wamba, in the Friar's robes, enters the castle and finds his way to Cedric. The two exchange outer garments.

In these chapters a new character, the ancient Saxon crone, Urfried (Ulrica), is introduced. Cedric, in the guise of a priest, converses with her and learns of her sordid past.

Front-de-Boeuf gives Cedric a message to be carried to Philip Malvoisin and a gold byzant in payment. Cedric throws the money toward the donor and joins the besiegers.

Wamba's disguise and Cedric's escape are discovered by Front-de-Boeuf and De Bracy. When the terms of the ransom are rejected by the prisoners, the storming of Torquilstone becomes imminent.

Commentary

Rebecca, usually docile and submissive, is aroused to noble defiance by the threat of the Templar. There is probably the beginning of a genuine regard for her as he says admiringly, "I do not say forgive me the violence I have threatened for it was necessary to the display of thy character. Gold can be only known by the application of the touchstone."

The courage of Rebecca, who would have thrown herself over the parapet before submitting to the proposal of the Knight Templar, is in sharp contrast with the earlier behavior of Ulrica, who had accepted dishonor rather than death. Note a later reference to the parapet scene, in which superstition gives a distorted view.

Through the Templar, Scott makes a statement about prejudice between Jew and Gentile which is significant in light of the general hostility toward the Jews, when Bois-Guilbert says in reply to Rebecca, "Answer me not by urging the difference in our creeds; within our secret conclaves we hold these nursery tales in derision."

As De Bracy and Bois-Guilbert discuss their unsuccessful suits, De Bracy compares Rowena's tears to those of "St. Niobe, of whom Prior Aymer told us." Niobe was not a saint but a pagan of Greek legend.

The letter, supposedly written by a fool and a swineherd is itself an affront and a joke of the Jolly Friar's.

The rescue team is, interestingly, composed of all those wronged by the Normans: the Saxons, the robber band, and the Black Knight.

The comic irony of the words, "Pax vobiscum" (Peace be with you) used by Wamba to gain entrance into the castle, is apparent because they are incongruous to the battle about to begin. Wamba makes the most of it when he instructs Cedric in their use.

The confession of Ulrica serves two purposes. It reveals her own guilt and the depravity of Front-de-Boeuf and his ancestors.

CHAPTERS 28-29

Summary

Scott uses a flashback to supply missing information about the wounded Ivanhoe from the time of the tournament until the battle of Torquilstone. When Rebecca gave up her litter to the invalid and exposed herself on horseback, Brian de Bois-Guilbert noted her beauty and desired her. Regaining consciousness, Ivanhoe was surprised to find himself in the company of the Jewess. She told him of her healing knowledge and promised to make him well in eight days. On the journey toward York Cedric's party overtook that of Isaac, and when all were captured by De Bracy, Ivanhoe was also taken to Torquilstone.

Ivanhoe is left in the care of Rebecca and when the fighting begins she, although in peril from the flying arrows and stones, stands at a window and describes the struggle to the wounded knight. As the besiegers appear to have won, Ivanhoe, exhausted from the excitement, falls asleep and Rebecca muses over her feeling for him.

Commentary

In introducing the flashback in Chapter 28, Scott again uses authorial intrusion — standing outside the novel to comment upon it as a contrived piece. The flashback in Chapter 28 typifies the time shifts throughout *Ivanhoe*. Scott is depicting the action by scenes, and if a scene involving one set of characters occurs simultaneously with a scene involving other characters of the novel, the author used flashbacks or time shifts to follow the fortunes of both sets of characters. At times this method leaves an impression of illogical time sequences.

The kindness of Isaac in allowing Rebecca to minister to Ivanhoe is somewhat overshadowed by the fact that he is persuaded because he doesn't want the knowledge of the healing balsam to fall into other hands and that it may profit him to have shown kindness to one of his minions should Richard return to power. Rebecca, however, who has received the secrets of Miriam, has no motive other than her natural goodness and an affection for Ivanhoe contrary to what she, as a Jewess, ought to feel for a Christian.

The biographer Henry A. Beers writes, "Scott is always a little nervous when the lover and the lady are left alone together." He cites an example from *The Lay of the Last Minstrel:*

> Now leave we Margaret and her knight
> To tell you of the approaching fight.

(Canto Fifth)

The reader will notice some of this also in *Ivanhoe.*

Chapter 29 includes an important dialogue involving the Jewess Rebecca and the Christian knight Ivanhoe. Ivanhoe is defending the medieval code of chivalry and honor to one who views it as a rationalization for bloodshed and empty trappings. Victory, renown, and glory are the ambitions of medieval knights, and disgrace is the only fate they fear. Ivanhoe's speech is pivotal in Scott's representation of the essence of chivalry.

CHAPTERS 30-31

Summary

Front-de-Boeuf, mortally wounded in the fighting, is reviled by Ulrica as he is dying. She rightfully accuses him of blasphemy and parricide, for she has witnessed the murder of his father. In a last desperate effort at revenge, Ulrica has set fire to the castle. Both she and Front-de-Boeuf perish in the flames.

Meanwhile the leadership of the besiegers has been divided between the Black Knight and Locksley. In the fighting the Black Knight captures De Bracy and saves Ivanhoe from the burning castle. All of the prisoners escape except Rebecca, who is carried off by the amorous Brian de Bois-Guilbert. In an attempt to stop the Templar, Athelstane receives a blow on the head and falls down as if dead.

Commentary

Animosity and distrust within the ranks of the Normans are apparent in these chapters. Front-de-Boeuf rather hopes to see De Bracy and Bois-Guilbert die along with the Saxons in the burning castle. Similarly, De Bracy and Bois-Guilbert discuss Front-de-Boeuf's death with equanimity and are only interested in its consequences for the cause of Prince John. They then accuse each other of superstition or heresy in regard to religion. Both condemn Fitzurse for incurring the enmity of Locksley.

The division of leadership is noteworthy in that Cedric declines to lead the Saxon forces. "Not so, by the soul of Hereward!, lead I cannot." The implication of lack of leadership ability may be one of the keys to the fall of Saxon dominion.

Ulrica's death song is an imitation of the poems of antiquity of the Scalds, Scandinavian minstrels. Ulrica probably learned these legendary strains from her Scandinavian ancestors. The death scene involving Ulrica is perhaps melodramatic but serves to intensify the background of superstition and legend which is a part of the novel.

CHAPTERS 32-34

Summary

The liberated party assemble at Locksley's trysting place in the forest, where Cedric makes Gurth a free man. Cedric refuses a share of the plunder from the castle, but both he and Rowena express gratitude for Locksley's help.

Friar Tuck arrives leading Isaac by a rope around his neck. The Friar and the Black Knight engage in friendly fisticuffs to decide the fate of the Jew. The Jew and the Prior set each other's ransom and Isaac learns of Rebecca's abduction. For a price the Prior offers to use his influence with Brian de Bois-Guilbert and furnishes a letter to this effect. The Saxon party leaves with the body of Athelstane to prepare the funeral rites at Coningsburgh Castle, Athelstane's home.

De Bracy, set free by the Black Knight, announces to Prince John that Richard is in England, that Bois-Guilbert has fled, and that Front-de-Boeuf is dead. When he recovers from the shock, Prince John conceives a plot to make his brother prisoner and Fitzurse sets out to do his bidding.

Commentary

In character, quote, or scene, Shakespeare was often present with Scott. Note the similarity between Isaac and Shylock of *The Merchant of Venice*. The forest scene of this chapter is reminiscent of *A Midsummer Night's Dream*. The robber band often has impish or elfin qualities, and further distinctions of a supernatural nature are introduced by references to "the Devil that is in his jerkin" and "mortal Men" (as opposed to immortal men).

That King Richard would stoop to an exchange of blows with the Friar is not unlikely. He was supposed to have had such an encounter when he was a prisoner in Germany. According to the story his antagonist was a warder's son. Richard received a hard blow and returned one with such force that he killed his adversary.

The complicated finagling about setting the ransom of the Prior and the Jew is included for the sake of its humor. A Jew is pitted against a churchman and a comic priest against a corrupt one. The outlaw mediator is the only one who shows principle. The equity with which Locksley divides the spoil illustrates the adage "honor among thieves."

Distrust and intrigue in officialdom is an old story. At the time of which Scott writes it often initiated a change of loyalty as a matter of saving one's own neck.

CHAPTERS 35-36

Summary

Isaac, bearing the letter from the Prior to Brian de Bois-Guilbert, arrives at Templestowe and is brought to the Grand

Master, Lucas Beaumanoir. The letter discloses Rebecca's presence at Templestowe and thus casts reflection on Brian de Bois-Guilbert. At the same time its contents (by insinuation) condemn Rebecca as a sorceress, "a second witch of Endor."

Albert Malvoisin, Preceptor of Templestowe, makes excuses for the Templar, claiming he has been enticed against his will. Meanwhile Bois-Guilbert, finding himself in love with her, has been pressing his suit with Rebecca, only to be repulsed. When Malvoisin reminds him of his ambitions in the order and how his concern with a Jewess is endangering his future, Brian de Bois-Guilbert is torn between two desires.

Beaumanoir orders an immediate trial to convict Rebecca as a witch. The Templar seeks a way to help her escape.

Commentary

Superstition and a fanatical hatred of Jews combine to hasten the trial of Rebecca. Lucas Beaumanoir, proud and forceful chief of the Templars, allows this to take precedence over any contempt for the Prior, or punishment for the Templar.

That greed for power had also invaded the ranks of the Templars is evident in Malvoisin's words to Bois-Guilbert, "Women are but the toys which amuse our lighter hours; ambition is the serious business of life." The "holy rule" which the Grand Master quotes in Latin is against loose women and, ironically, does not apply to the virtuous Rebecca.

CHAPTERS 37-39

Summary

At Rebecca's trial the charges against Brian de Bois-Guilbert are read and tempered by the intimation that he was made devoid of reason by a supernatural power.

Witnesses against Rebecca testify to her occult powers of healing and curious happenings concerning her appearance on the parapet at the storming of Torquilstone. Her beauty and innocent defense affect the crowd, but have little bearing on the outcome of the trial. At Brian de Bois-Guilbert's prompting she demands a champion to represent her in trial by combat and gains a reprieve. A peasant is sent at once to Isaac so that he may seek a champion. Bois-Gulbert, sensing that a champion may not be found, urges her her to elope with him.

Commentary

The student of American history and literature will detect in the Salem witchcraft trials echoes of the trumped-up charges against Rebecca. Rebecca is condemned both by the lies of witnesses against her and for following certain customs common to the Jews but which appear strange to Christian Englishmen. In their strangeness, to the audience of the tribunal they seem to suggest sacrilege. The audience construe difference in manners as proof of evil.

It is difficult to hold Bois-Guilbert in complete contempt as he begins to show some admirable qualities. His immoral intentions pale somewhat in his attempts to protect Rebecca. Rebecca's character is consistent in her firm rejection of all Bois-Guilbert's proposals. Rebecca is heard to say of the Templar, "I envy thee not thy faith, which is ever in thy mouth but never in thy heart nor in thy practice." This is fine assessment of many religious groups.

CHAPTERS 40-42

Summary

On their way to Athelstane's castle of Coningsburgh, the Black Knight and Wamba are attacked by Waldemar Fitzurse and his men. With the help of Robin Hood and his band, called up by the horn, Richard slays all of his enemies except Fitzurse, whom he banishes from England. Richard's magnanimity toward his brother John is shown in his command that Prince John's name not be mentioned in connection with the attack just made on his life.

In Chapter 40 the Black Knight reveals himself as Richard to those present. When Ivanhoe and Gurth join the group they are all invited to be the guests of the outlaws.

King Richard and Ivanhoe and their party travel on to Conings-burgh, where the funeral feast for Athelstane is in progress. Athel-stane, who has only been knocked unconscious, appears, but before he can finish the story of his bizarre escape from the coffin, Ivanhoe is summoned to defend Rebecca.

Commentary

The roundelay which is sung by the Black Knight and Wamba in dialogue was the type of thing done by the rustics in their pas-torals. Its fun derives partly from the incongruity of being sung by a king and a fool.

This is not only the final revelation of Richard the Lion-Hearted, but a revelation of Locksley as the famous Robin Hood as well. According to legend, a village by the name of Locksley in Notting-hamshire was the birthplace of Robin Hood and he sometimes as-sumed this pseudonym when he affected disguise.

In this section some of the less desirable aspects of the char-acter King Richard are brough into focus. He is reckless to the point of indiscretion, "In the lion-hearted king...the personal glory which he acquired by his own deeds of arms was far more dear to his excited imagination than that which a course of policy and wis-dom would have spread around his government." He is quick to anger; "they who jest with Majesty even in its gayest mood, are but toying with the lion's whelp, which, on slight provocation, uses both fangs and claws."

The castle of Coningsburgh is one of the last remaining ex-amples of Saxon fortification. It probably belonged to King Harold and was given to William de Warren by William the Conqueror. The description of the castle and of the funeral feast is unparalleled in sharpness and accuracy of detail.

In the interest of keeping the historical record straight, Scott somewhat dims the plot by telling of the demise of King Ricahrd and Prince John's accession to the throne.

While the "raising" of Athelstane is somewhat ludicrous, the section serves several ends. Most important is the forging of a final link in the gradual, but relentless, breakdown of Saxon resistance to Norman rule. This was begun by Ivanhoe when he left his father's home to fight by the side of King Richard and reinforced by the lack of leadership which Cedric displayed at a moment of crisis. Significant to the story is Athelstane's obeisance to King Richard and his relinquishing Rowena to Ivanhoe.

CHAPTERS 43-44

Summary

Many people assemble at Templestowe for the combat which is to decide the fate of Rebecca. Among them are Allan-a-Dale and Friar Tuck, who discuss the legend which is rapidly arising around Athelstane.

Brian de Bois-Guilbert, the unwilling champion of the order against Rebecca, appeals once more to her to ride away with him. With her customary disdain, she refuses. Just as it appears that no champion will appear to defend Rebecca, Ivanhoe rides into the lists. He and his horse are exhausted from the hard ride and, at the first skirmish, Ivanhoe is unseated. However, the Templar also falls to the ground, having died, "a victim to the violence of his own contending passions."

Rowena and Wilfred of Ivanhoe are married and it is to Rowena that Rebecca pays a final visit to tender her thanks for deliverance. She and her father leave England to live in Granada.

Commentary

The sudden death of Bois-Guilbert allows Ivanhoe to remain a credible hero. At the same time the Templar escapes disgrace, the only fate a knight fears, as Ivanhoe once told Rebecca. *Ivanhoe* is often called a fairy story. In the "Afterward" Compton Mackenzie says of it, "It may be a fairy story, but what a glorious fairy story it is!"

Rebecca apparently chooses to express her thanks and farewells to Lady Rowena rather than to Wilfred because she is afraid of revealing too much of her feelings to Ivanhoe. Scott has this comment about the ending:

> The character of the fair Jewess found so much favour in the eyes of some fair readers, that the writer was censured because when arranging the fates of the characters of the drama, he had not assigned the hand of Wilfred to Rebecca, rather than the less interesting Rowena. But not to mention that the prejudice of the age rendered such a union almost impossible, the Author may in passing observe, that he thinks a character of a highly virtuous and lofty stamp is degraded rather than exalted by an attempt to reward virtue with temporal prosperity. Such is not the recompense which Providence has deemed worthy of suffering merit, and it is a dangerous and fatal doctrine to teach young persons, the most common readers of romance, that rectitude of conduct and of principle are naturally allied with or adequately rewarded by the gratification of our passions, or attainment of our wishes.

CHARACTER SKETCHES

The characters in Ivanhoe are static. Except for minor changes in attitude, there is very little character development. They are mainly interesting as types having certain distinguishing characteristics. Wilfred of Ivanhoe represents the all-good personality and Front-de-Boeuf typifies the all-evil character. Somewhere between these one-dimensional figures is Brian de Bois-Guilbert.

WILFRED OF IVANHOE

Wilfred, often referred to simply as Ivanhoe, is the strong-willed son of a strong-willed father. He attaches himself to the lion-hearted king and follows him courageously into battle in the Crusades in Palestine. He enjoys a good fight. His love for his lady is constant. Although Scott raises a question in regard to his feeling for Rebecca, his love for Rowena is never seriously in question. He is brave, loyal to God and country, and has respect for his father, although he has been disowned.

LADY ROWENA

She is the female counterpart of Wilfred. She bears herself in a queenly fashion and has a will to match that of her guardian, Cedric the Saxon. Her love for Ivanhoe and her fear for his safety stir her emotionally more than is customary to her normal placidity.

She is beautiful, chaste, and always discreet. She forgives Maurice de Bracy because it is her duty "as a Christian," which Wamba says slyly, "means she doesn't forgive him at all." She is as magnanimous toward Rebecca as she is adamant toward Cedric's attempts to coerce her into marriage with Athelstane.

CEDRIC THE SAXON

The Saxon patriarch has more interest in re-establishing Saxon rule than in perpetuating his own house. When Wilfred disappoints him by falling in love with his ward, Rowena, and in swearing allegiance to King Richard Plantagenet, Cedric disinherits him.

Cedric has fierce pride in his nationality and chafes under Norman rule. Although he presents a rough exterior, he often betrays a kind heart. He observes the rules of hospitality even toward those he considers his enemies, but relents only momentarily toward reconciliation with his son, until his hope of Saxon rule is gone. He is slow to think and this, together with his crude speech, often puts him at disadvantage with the more polished Normans.

ATHELSTANE THE UNREADY

Slow to think and act, but brave and steady when aroused, with an insatiable appetite for food—this characterizes the "noble"

Saxon. He accepts the arrangement of the marriage to Rowena more because of pride and expediency than from any involvement of the heart, so that when he gives her up it is a matter of no great concern. He is often a comic figure and never more so than when he is describing his escape from the coffin.

REBECCA

Rebecca is beautiful and chaste, but her affection for Ivanhoe is unruly and unwise. She is so hard on Brian de Bois-Guilbert that one is constrained to feel sorry for the villain. She has strong religious faith, but it does not reduce her to stoicism. She "shudders" at her impending fate. Her innate kindness causes her to use her healing knowledge indiscriminately, but she suffers from the disclosure of the source. It is precisely these "human" qualities that cause some readers to prefer her to Rowena.

Rebecca was drawn from a real Jewess, Rebecca Gratz, who lived in Philadelphia, Pennsylvania. Washington Irving told Scott about her beauty and nobility of character.

ISAAC THE JEW

Isaac is a typical Jew, or more correctly, he is representative of a literary type. The "typical Jew" was portrayed as avaricious and obsequious unless he gained power over others; then he could be demanding and imperious. Isaac shares these tendencies but he can be kind, as to Ivanhoe when Ivanhoe is disguised as the Palmer and in need of equipage for the tournament.

Isaac loves two things, his daughter and his money. There always seems to be a struggle when the two are involved in the same transaction. The loss of money is the terrible price he pays for the greater love he bears his daughter.

PRINCE JOHN

Prince John is an injudicious, arrogant, petulant, suspicious, and conniving man whose bravery is always in question. He trusts no one, as the spy-upon-spy episode toward the end of the narrative indicates. He lives in fear of his brother's return, although more from fear of loss of power than from any danger to his person. When he tells De Bracy, "I seek no safety for myself, that I could secure by a word spoken to my brother," it is not all bravado. It proved to be true. King Richard took no action against his brother at all. In turn, John only seeks imprisonment for Richard. It is Fitzurse who threatens the king's life.

Those closest to him have no respect for him and maintain loyalty only for their own ambitious ends. He revels in the acclaim of the crowds and in a display of power. He appears to delight in setting one faction upon another.

KING RICHARD COEUR DE LION

Richard commands the allegiance of many kinds of people. Ivanhoe follows him to Palestine, Friar Tuck fraternizes with him, Wamba travels and sings with him, and the outlaw band entertain him at a meal. His brother fears his return, for the rumor that he may have returned is enough to turn his former subjects away from Prince John.

He sometimes shows a bad temper and a lack of good judgment, as at the revel in the forest, and traces of the arrogance of his brother are also apparent in King Richard. However, he is never lacking in courage and is forceful, as well as popular, with those whom he rules. He deals with his enemies without fear and, except for his brother, without favor.

WALDEMAR FITZURSE

Fitzurse, "wily politician" and adviser to Prince John, serves as conciliator for the arrogant and unwise leader. He mollifies the people whom Prince John insults and wins back those whose loyalties stray. He has a driving ambition to become chancellor to Prince John if the prince can usurp the throne. Although his advice is for the prince's good, it is his own welfare about which he is most concerned.

MAURICE DE BRACY

The dashing young Norman has more valor and love of life than good judgment. He is ambitious for a place in Prince John's court, unscrupulous in achieving these ends, and brave in battle, as shown by his part in defending Torquilstone. He accepts defeat without debasing himself. He is realistic about the effect of Richard's return and escapes hastily to France and a place in the court of Philip.

FRONT-DE-BOEUF

The "ox-faced" lord is as repellent as his name implies. His brutality is apparent as he torments Isaac in the basement of the palace and in the taunts of Ulrica as he is dying. His closest associates calmly discuss his death only in terms of the loss to Prince John's cause.

BRIAN DE BOIS-GUILBERT

The haughty Templar is a striking figure and a bold, though unprincipled, knight. His Saracen slaves attest to his subjugation of one people while seeking to advance the cause of another. He meets his match in Ivanhoe and the disgrace is damaging to his pride.

That Bois-Guilbert is not all evil is evidenced by Rebecca's judgment of him: "There are noble things which cross over thy powerful mind; but it is the garden of the sluggard, and the weeds have rushed up, and conspired to choke the fair and wholesome blossom." He is caught in the web of his own licentious making as his desire for Rebecca wars with his ambitions in the order of Knights Templar. His death is the result of his unresolved passions.

PRIOR AYMER OF JORVAULX

The Prior uses the office of the church to line his own pockets and as a shield for practicing vice. He caters to the Normans, but can trace some Saxon blood in his lineage if it is necessary to keep in the good graces of Cedric. The impious priest is a part of the corrupt picture of the medieval church that Scott was painting.

LUCAS BEAUMANOIR

The Grand Master of the Templars is an "ascetic bigot," a "formidable warrior," and yet has something "striking and noble" about him. He is stripped of his piety by the quick and heartless condemnation of Rebecca. He is affected by her demeanor and protestations of innocence, but this is dispelled by the fact that she is a member of a hated race and that her presence casts reflection upon one of the knights of his order.

Scott adopts an ironic succession of attitudes when he has Beaumanoir condemn the knights and priests for their lack of attention to their holy vows and then impose such inhumane treatment on the helpless girl.

LOCKSLEY (ROBIN HOOD)

Robin Hood, alias Locksley, rollicking king of the forest outlaws, is a legendary figure who allegedly robbed the rich to give to the poor. He represents defiance against law and order and helps the "good" or "better" against the wicked. He is skilled in archery and lives by being quick-witted and daring.

THE CLERK OF COPMANHURST (FRIAR TUCK)

Friar Tuck, the outlaw priest, is more outlaw than priest. He is more adept at fighting than in speaking Latin. He is, however one of a type of "holy" men, called Hedge Priests, who performed perverted religious rites for men of doubtful character. The Hedge Priests had morals to match those of the men they served. The Friar in *Ivanhoe,* however, is more comic than evil.

WAMBA

Wamba is a delightful character whose wit is his stock-in-trade. It is a tribute to Scott's genius that Wamba has just the right amount of loyalty to Cedric and his friends, as well as a sense of pithy good humor. He is able to insert a pointed remark at the right time by the audacity allowed a jester.

GURTH

The swineherd may resemble the rustic of Scott's own day, but he is a believable person with real fears, a homely disposition, and mixed loyalties. His presence makes possible the rite of raising a bondsman to the status of freedman.

ULRICA (URFRIED)

In spite of the wrongs which have been done to Ulrica, she appears more as a witch than a woman. Her guilt in consorting with the Norman lords allows sympathy to rise for her only momentarily. She provides a dramatic climax to the destruction of the palace of Torquilstone as she chants her death song from the turret.

STYLE

Sir Walter Scott is a storytelling author. The story is in third person, but when he wishes to explain something to the reader he breaks in and resorts to first person. His point of view is of one watching an exciting drama and relaying what he sees with suitable explanation so that none of the excitement is lost.

He uses a disjointed flashback. He carries the action of one group to a certain point and then goes back to pick up another group to bring it into logical position. It is as though he were weaving together varied colored threads into one exquisite pattern. It is his task to put the threads together so that the finished piece of cloth is one carefully wrought, panoramic scene. Foremost are the figures, often in violent action, against a background of vivid natural beauty. To miss the description is to rob the piece of its wholeness and to be impatient with the archaic and distinctive words is to destroy the medieval setting.

He gives structural clues to move the story along, such as Rebecca's warning of robbers to Gurth, which prepares the reader for the swineherd's encounter with the thieves; Fang's howling precipitates the capture by De Bracy; the phrase which the Prior drops, "the witch of Endor," signifies Rebecca's trial.

HISTORY, ROMANTICISM, RELIGION

HISTORY

Scott's formula for the historical novel was an unmistakable innovation which became a pattern for those who followed him. His story is pure fiction, his hero is imaginary. For example, it is Ivanhoe who is the hero, not Richard Coeur de Lion; the setting is as authentic as possible, and the events of history are quite accurate. As Henry Beers says, "He possessed the true enchanter's wand, the historic imagination. With this in his hand he raised the dead past to life, made it once more conceivable, made it even actual."[1]

Furthermore, he made history romantic, and to those who feel history to be dull, he makes it exciting. Many authors have written histories more accurate in detail and with more attention to chronology; some have written romances more tender and ethereal, but no one combines history and romance and makes them both more lovely and believable.

Scott read history with an avidity probably unequaled by any novelist so that, although he was sometimes careless, his work is authentic in spite of it. He loved scenery only when it had a castle or a battle site which related it to history. Where this happy combination resulted he fashioned a story. His friend Mr. Morritt of Rokesbury said of him, "He was but half-satisfied with the most beautiful scenery when he could not connect it with some local legend."[2]

In his historical romances in general, and in *Ivanhoe* in particular, Scott captured the spirit of the age; he imitated the speech, the

---

[1]Henry A. Beers, *A History of English Romanticism* (New York, 1901), p. 38.
[2]Beers, p. 18.

rude humor, the customs, and reconstructed a past age until it became a living present. He did not go deep into the cause of a historical event, just as he did not go deep into spiritualities, or men's thoughts, but he described in vivid detail and told a whopping good story. More particularly in *Ivanhoe* he was not always accurate, but he did more for the medieval era historically than almost anyone else to make it a part of the body of knowledge.

It is with the description of battles and the external aspects of knighthood, the outlaws bands, and the Norman-Saxon conflict that Scott is especially interesting. He is never satirical and only mildly ironic, but he has a verve for color and action that is his specialty. Only at times, when he interrupts his story to add extraneous material, is the reader led away from the action.

One writer sees historical value in the treatment of the smoldering hatred by the Saxon for the Normans which was brought into harmony and finally dissolved under King Richard. He also believes that the account of the brothers Richard and John is quite accurate, except that King Richard was probably less gallant than he appears here. He allows the bigotry of the Grand Master of the Templars and discredits the love of Bois-Guilbert for the Jewess as highly improbable.[3]

Another point of historical interest is the resemblance of Shakespeare's King John to the Prince John of *Ivanhoe*. That Scott was indeed a student of Shakespeare is evident from the many quotes from Shakespeare's plays.

Scott drew heavily on Shakespeare as well as Chaucer. Isaac and Rebecca hark back to Shylock and Jessica of the *Merchant of Venice*. Wamba resembles the fools of *King Lear, Twelfth Night,* and *As You Like It*. Richard I has the qualities of a national leader found in *Henry V*. Even the device of a funeral for one not dead can be traced to *Cymbeline* and *Romeo and Juliet;* Athelstane echoes Cloten.

[3] Albert S. G. Canning, *History in Scott's Novels* (New York: A. Wessels Co., 1907).

Ivanhoe marks a departure from the Scottish themes employed by Scott prior to the year 1819. He felt that he was exhausting his material and that he needed a change of scene. As a result he produced a masterpiece that has influenced most tales of derring-do written since.

ROMANTICISM

Since Scott's writings are historical romances, romanticism and history are hardly separable. His passion for places made it easy for him to romanticize the events that took place there. In regard to his poem, *The Lay of the Last Minstrel,* in which romanticism is said to have arrived, Henry Beers expresses the wish that "Collins and Tom Wharton might have lived to hail it as the light at last, towards which they had struggled through the cold obstruction of the eighteenth century. One fancies Dr. Johnson's disgust over this new monstrosity which had every quality he disliked except blank verse; or Gray's delight in it, tempered by a critical disapproval of its loose construction and irregularity."[4]

Scott was interested in superstition, which was in vogue in romantic literature, but only as a curiosity. Someone once said something to the effect that he saw too much daylight through the dark mysticism to be much affected by it. His use of superstition is certainly more romantic than with any intent to make it credulous.

RELIGION

Although knights are important in *Ivanhoe,* the Crusades are merely referred to. In one instance, however, the Grand Master seems to blame priests such as Prior Aymer and some of the Templars for the loss of the Holy Land by Christians, "place by place, foot by foot, before the infidels."

The Catholic church suffers indignity by the character of Prior Aymer. The Dutch writer Bos says he is a "character revolting to true Catholics."[5] Friar Tuck on the other hand, is not a true priest,

[4]Beers, p. 28.
[5]Klaas Box, *Religious Creeds and Philosophies as Represented by Characters in Sir Walter Scott's Works and Biography* (Amsterdam, 1932).

or is considered an "unfrocked one" by most Catholics and therefore not a reflection upon the church.

Although Scott came in for some abuse for his treatment of the Catholic church, most Catholics have long since written off his characters as caricatures having little to do with the faith, and his scenes such as the funeral rites of Athelstane as burlesque.

Scott's Jew as depicted in Isaac is typical of the stereotyped member of a race hated for his usury and more particularly for his religion, since the Christian Crusaders were incensed against anyone who was an unbeliever in Christ as the messiah. They laid at the door of any Jew the responsibility for Christ's crucifixion. Antisemitism today, although stemming from the same root, has lost most of the religious context.

The Jew as shown by Rebecca, her comments, and religious fervor, is certainly more sympathetic. Wamba also makes pithy observations; for example in a saucy retort to the haughty Templar, he says, "By my faith, it would seem the Templars love the Jews' inheritance better than they do their company," which raises the estimation of Jews and warrants a second look by Christian readers.

The love interest of Rebecca and Wilfred is unlikely, as is the kindly attitude of Rowena toward the Jewess. The close contact would probably never have taken place, and as one author puts it, "is probably true only in the kindness of Scott's own heart."[6]

SCOTT AND SCOTLAND

"O Scotia! my dear, my native soil! For whom my warmest wish to Heaven is sent."

Robert Burns: "A Cotter's Saturday Night"

[6]Beers, p. 18.

Scotland today advertises itself to tourists as the land of Scott and Burns. Different as the two great romantic authors were in personality and literary achievement as well as in social position, both were thoroughly Scotch. Scott was well-to-do, Burns poor. Scott was a nobleman, Burns a peasant. To use his own words, Scott could do "the big bow-wow strain" of stirring narrative and historical romance.

Sir Walter Scott was a native of Edinburgh. A marker in Guthrie Street bears this inscription: "Near this spot stood the house in which Sir Walter Scott was born." On Princes' Street, one of the most beautiful avenues in the world, with buildings only on one side and the hills on the other side sloping up to Holyrood and Edinburgh castles, is an elaborate monument to Sir Walter and his dog. Edinburgh is the scene of *The Heart of Midlothian* (the old prison and Jeanie Deans's cottage are still standing); *Guy Mannering,* the tale of an astrologer's prophecy and a boy kidnaped by gypsies; *Old Mortality,* dealing with the rise of Presbyterianism in Scotland; *Redgauntlet;* and *The Abbot.* Yet Scott loved the Lowlands, too, for there was his home, Abbotsford, where he lived like a feudal lord until financial disaster overtook him.

The River Tweed winds through Melrose district, past Dryburgh and Melrose Abbeys and Abbotsford itself. Sir Walter's view of the Tweed, where on the crest of a hill he had trained his horses to stop and had trained them so thoroughly that they stopped with his funeral cortege, may be compared on this side of the Atlantic with Thomas Jefferson's view from Monticello. Jefferson, however, could see no river.

Approaching Abbotsford, the tourist may encounter a bagpipe player, gay in Scotch tartan, his instrument emitting strains thought to be those of "Hail to the Chief," from *The Lady of the Lake.* In the study where the lame but terrifically energetic novelist often worked three hours before breakfast in order to clear Abbotsford of debt, he would grind out chapters of *Ivanhoe* or *The Talisman,* hiding them in a drawer when visitors came in. A little gallery around all four walls of the study is reached by a tiny staircase. Walls, gallery, and ground floor alike are lined with books, many of them Sir

Walter's own. The next room is the main library, with 20,000 volumes collected by the author himself. Here are family portraits, including a famous painting of Scott and his dog and first editions of *The Lady of the Lake, The Lay of the Last Minstrel,* and *Minstrelsy of the Scottish Border.* In a glass case are relics mentioned in the novels.

In other rooms are such treasures as the swords described in *Rob Roy,* the keys to the Heart of Midlothian, and the Lochleven key, thrown into the lake after the escape of Mary, Queen of Scots, and retrieved later. Pictures of Tom Purdie and Mucklemouth Meg are also there, as well as Scott's shoes, top hat, and plaid suit of black and white.

Amid the ruins of Dryburgh Abbey is the simple grave of the great novelist, as well as those of his wife and his faithful son-in-law, Lockhart. Kelso and Jedburgh are also associated with Scott, and so is Selkirk, where he was sheriff of the shire. Melrose Abbey, loveliest ruin in Scotland, is the scene of *The Lay of the Last Minstrel.*

> If you would see fair Melrose aright
> Go visit it by the pale moonlight,

wrote Scott. Not many miles away are the Lammermoor Hills, associated with the tragic fate of the Bride of Lammermoor, Lucy Ashton. Just north of Berwick-on-Tweed is "Norham's castled steep" of *Marmion,* and south of the river is Flodden Field.

Scott was the first British novelist to make a background studied from nature an essential element of his work. Although his tales may lead us to medieval France, like *Quentin Durward,* or central England, like *Ivanhoe,* or Jerusalem, like *The Talisman,* the majority of them are Scottish, projected against the background of the author's native land. The vogue for historical fiction which Scott started has spread on both sides of the ocean. *Gone With the Wind, Drums Along the Mohawk,* and *Northwest Passage* are samples of the literary descendants of *Kenilworth, Quentin Durward,* and *Ivanhoe.*

SCOTT AND THE AMERICAN SOUTH

Some notes more pertinent to our own times and country are contained in a book by a contemporary historian, John Hope Franklin. Dr. Franklin writes,

> Among the writers with a considerable following in the South, Sir Walter Scott is regarded by many as a leader. How extensively and what influence he wielded are difficult questions to answer. Some contend that the Scott novels were the Bible's only competitors for the attention of literate Southerners, that their martial and chivalric themes became the rule of life.

In another instance he says:

> Such works reflected the old ideals of fine lords and ladies which Southerners now set themselves to imitate and reflect. Scott doubtless bolstered the social philosophy that gradually came to dominate the section. He also excited the imagination of those who, either in splendid or wretched isolation pursued a vicarious existence through the colorful pages of *Ivanhoe*.

In the same book, Dr. Franklin, who is seeking to establish the social relationships of that unhappy land, quotes from Mark Twain and H. J. Eckenrode. Twain said of Scott:

> But for the Sir Walter Scott disease the character of the Southerner — or Southron, according to Sir Walter Scott's starchier way of phrasing it — would be wholly modern, in place of modern and medieval mixed. . . . It was Sir Walter Scott that made every gentleman in the South a major or a colonel, or, a general or a judge, before the war; and it was he also that made these gentlemen value these bogus decorations. . . . Sir Walter had so large a hand in making Southern character, as it existed before the war, that he is in great measure responsible for the war.

Eckenrode, hardly less vitriolic, wrote,

> Beyond doubt Scott gave the South its social ideal, and the South of 1860 might not be inaptly nicknamed Sir Walter Scottland. He did not create the state of feeling which held

sway in the South so long, but he gave it expression.... The term Southern Chivalry, unknown in the colonial period, came into use through his influence.[6]

Thus Scott receives some doubtful fame in our own country. Perhaps the unfavorable influence was not so much in the author of fanciful tales, but in a people who were looking for a way to elevate themselves to a place where they could think of themselves more "highly than they ought to think." Certainly it was not in the mind of Scott to make a pattern for a way of life when he peopled his stories with the "lords and ladies of medieval times."

GLOSSARY

Chapter 1

hauberk	a coat of mail developed into a long tunic of chain mail; part of medieval armor
druidical	having to do with members of a religious order in ancient Gaul, Britain, and Ireland
harlequin	a character in a comedy and pantomime having shaven head, masked face, particolored tights, and a sword of lath
St. Dunstan	Saxon saint and archbishop of Canterbury in the tenth century
King Oberon	fairy king in Shakespeare's *A Midsummer Night's Dream*
murrain	a pestilence or plague
Eumaeus	swineherd in Homer's *Odyssey*

[6]John Hope Franklin, *The Militant South* (Cambridge: Harvard University Press, 1956), pp. 193-96.

Chapter 2

damascene	to decorate, as iron or steel, with a peculiar marking or "water" produced in the manufacture
el jerrid	a javelin used in Oriental games, especially in mock-fights on horseback
Benedicite, mes filz	Bless you my children.

Chapter 3

choleric	producing biliousness
doublet	a close-fitting jacket
morat	drink made of honey flavored with the juice of mulberries
pigments	highly spiced wine sweetened with honey
dais	a platform above the floor of a large room
chian	wine of Chios, an island of Asia Minor
lac dulce	sweet milk
lac acidum	sour milk

Chapter 5

recheat	a signal to the hounds to return from following a false scent
mort	a bugle call at the death of a stag
curee	the portion of the deer given to the hounds
arbor	the pluck of the deer
nombles	the entrails of the deer

cri de guerre	war cry
grace-cup	a cup used in drinking a final health after the grace at the end of a meal, or a health drunk from it
shekel	an ancient weight and money unit, or coin. Hebrew shekel for gold about 252 2/3 grains (about $10.88)
halfling	the half of a silver penny

Chapter 6

solere	a garret or upper chamber
benison	blessing, benediction
matins	morning prayers
lazarus	Biblical beggar
gammon	a ham or lower half of bacon side, smoked or dried
buckram	coarse cloth
en croupe	behind the saddle

Chapter 7

La Royne de Beaulte et des Amours	the Queen of Beauty and of Love
caracoled	half turn to the right and half turn to the left, zigzagged
maroquin	Morroco, goat's leather
simarre	a woman's light, loose robe
hinds	peasants
byzants	a Byzantine gold coin

Chapter 8

halidom	holiness, sanctity; sanctuary, holy relics
largesse	a gift
cap-a-pie	from head to foot
escutcheons	the surface of a shield where armorial bearings are displayed
Gare le corbeau	Beware of the raven.
Cave, adsum	Beware, I am here.

Chapter 9

Wot ye?	What do you think? What do you know?
donative	gift or present
outrecuidance	insolence, presumption

Chapter 10

zecchins	a Venetian coin, about 9s.4d.
varlet	attendant, servant
estrada	a slightly raised platform
talents	a unit of money, worth about 50 Hebrew shekels

Chapter 11

arrant	notoriously or pre-eminently bad
faire le moulinet	to twirl about, flourish a quarter staff

Chapter 12

Laissez aller!	Let go! Away!

Chapter 13

fleurs-de-lis	heraldic lilies
bucklers	kinds of shields worn on one of the arms to protect the front of the body
chamberlain	a steward

Chapter 14

purveyors	caterers, officers who exact provisions
objurgations	denouncement
karum pie	a pie containing nightingales and beccaficoes (blackcaps)
nidering	infamous, base, cowardly

Chapter 15

primogeniture	firstborn child of the same parents

Chapter 16

anchorite	one who renounces the world to live in seclusion
Shadrach, Meshech, Abednego	Bible characters who abstained from the heathen king's meat and drink
stoup	a small cask
runlet	a small barrel
Waes hael.	To your health.
Drinc Hael.	I drink your health.

Chapter 17

derry-down chorus	chorus to the hymns of the Druids
exceptis excipiendis	except what is to be excepted

Chapter 18

rere-supper	late night meal after the regular meal

Chapter 19

baldric	a belt worn over the shoulder to support a sword or bugle
vizard	mask or visor

Chapter 20

yeoman	in this case freeborn men, or freedmen
De profundis clamavi.	Out of the depths have I called.
nocturnal potations	night of drinking
transmew	change

Chapter 21

peccadillo	slight offenses; petty faults
refectories	dining halls in a monastery or convent

Chapter 22

patrimony	an estate inherited from one's father or other ancestor

Chapter 23

loadstar (lodestar)	a star that leads, especially the polestar
physiognomists	persons who attempt to discover temperament by the outward appearance, especially of the face

Chapter 24

sibyl	prophetess; fortune-teller

unguent	a salve for sores, burns, or the like; ointment
alembic	an apparatus formerly used in distillation
Despardieux!	By God!
par amours	illicitly, unlawfully
ecclesiastica	woman devoted to religion, or to the church
embrasure	a recess of door or window (machicolles)

Chapter 25

cnichts	according to Saxon usage a class of military attendants ranking above the ordinary domestic; now spelled "knight" and ranking with Norman chevalier
Pax vobiscum.	Peace be with you.

Chapter 26

Et vobis; quoeso, Domine Reverendissime, pro misericordia vestra	And with you; O most reverend master, I beseech you, in your mercy.
Odin	Norse god of war; of those slain in battle; and of wisdom, and of poetry
Thor	Norse god of thunder, god of strength, and helper in war

Chapter 27

complaisance	disposition to please or oblige

sallyport	a rear gate, or an underground passage
surquedy	insolence, or presumption
biggin	child's cap
witenagemotes	the Anglo-Saxon great council or parliament
Deus vobiscum	God be with you; a priest
si quis, suadente diabolo	If anyone at the persuasion of the devil
mantelets	temporary and movable defenses formed of planks
pavisses	species of large shields covering the whole person

Chapter 28

caftaned	wearing a long-sleeved gown fastened by a girdle (a caftan)
slot-hounds	a sleuth hound, bloodhound
Shylock	Jew in Shakespeare's *Merchant of Venice*
truncheon	a short staff or cudgel
arblast	crossbow

Chapter 29

A la rescousee.	To the rescue.
assoilize	absolve

Chapter 30

malapert	bold, impudent; saucy, pert
unhouseled	not having had the Eucharist administered

hengist, or hengst	means stallion, the white horse as Saxon ensign

Chapter 31

partizan	any member of a military body harassing an enemy
Mount Joye Saint Denis	a war cry of the French Crusaders
Zernebock	the black god or Devil of the Wends and Prussian Slavs

Chapter 32

Aldhelm of Malmsbury	a scholar and church-builder of the seventh century
theow and esne	thrall and bondsman
levin-fire	lightning
quondam	having been formerly; former; sometime

Chapter 33

manus imponere in servos Domini	to lay hands on the servant of the Lord
Excommunicabo vos.	I will excommunicate you.
nebulo quidam	good for nothing fellow, scamp
pouncet-box	a box for carrying pomander (perfume)
crisping-tongs	curling iron
Watling Street	an old Roman road from Dover to the neighborhood of Newcastle-on-Tyne
propter necessitatem et ad frigus depellendum	in case of necessity and to drive away the cold

latro famosus	famous robber
phalanx	body of troops closely arrayed (here, birds)
inter res sacras	accounted sacred

Chapter 34

gibbets	a kind of gallows where malefactors were left hanging as a warning
Clifford's Gate	in Clifford's Tower (did not exist in Richard's reign)
Sir Guy	the hero of a medieval romance
Sir Bevis	of Hampton, a hero of a medieval romance
Tracy, Morville, Brito	slayers of Thomas-a-Becket

Chapter 35

Ut leo semper feriatur.	Let the lion always be beaten down.
Ut omnium mulierum fugiantur oscula.	Let all kissing be avoided.
de lectione literarum	on the reading of letters
Vinum loetificat cor hominis.	Wine maketh glad the heart of man.
Rex delectabitur pulchritucine tua.	The king shall rejoice in thy beauty.
Semper percutiatur leo.	The ravening lion is ever to be beaten down.

Chapter 36

de commilitonibus Templi in sancta civitate, qui cum miserrimis mulieribus versantur, propter oblectationem carnis	concerning the brethren in arms of the holy community of the Temple who frequent the company of misguided women for the gratification of their fleshly lusts

le don d'smoutrux merci   the highest favor that love can bestow

Chapter 37

Auferte malum ex vobis.   Remove the evil from among you.

cabalistic   pertaining to mystic symbols

Chapter 38

essoine   in this case, excuse

capul   horse

phlebotomy   the practice of opening a vein for the letting of blood

Chapter 39

exorcism   the act of driving off evil spirits

Chapter 40

destrier   war horse

Fructus Temporum   *The Chronicles of England with the Fruit of the Times*

pursy   short-winded because of overweight

morion   a foot soldier's visor-less high crested helmet

Confiteor.   I confess.

crosier   the staff of a bishop or abbot, shaped like a shepherd's crook

Chapter 41

heathenesse	heathenism; heathendom
panegyric	eulogistic oration

Chapter 42

Woden, or Odin	the chief god of ancient Teutonic mythology
soul-scat	a funeral due paid to the church
Mort de ma vie!	Death of my life!
oubliette	a dungeon, deep pit or shaft in a dungeon
tregetour	conjuror

Chapter 43

flints	men of the right sort
dunghills	lowbred fellows
te igitur	the servicebook, on which oaths were sworn
reliquary	small box, casket, or shrine for keeping a relic
Faites vos devoirs, preux chevaliers.	Do your duty, brave knights.
Fiat voluntas tua.	Thy will be done.

Chapter 44

Quare fremeurunt gentes?	Why do the heathen rage?

EXAMINATION AND REVIEW QUESTIONS

Note: The references in parentheses will help in answering the questions.

1. Give the time, setting, and chief characters of *Ivanhoe*.

2. Comment on how *Ivanhoe* and the other Scott novels have influenced modern literature in regard to (a) use of a historical background, (b) rapid action and adventure, (c) feats of skill and strength, (d) beauty in distress, and (e) display of moral as well as physical courage.

3. List examples of the following devices: (a) kidnaping, (b) disguise, (c) reference to witchcraft or the supernatural, and (d) banishment.

4. Comment on Scott's indebtedness to Shakespeare and Chaucer in the writing of *Ivanhoe*.

5. Comment on Scott's style in regard to (a) word choice, (b) length of sentences and type of punctuation, (c) vividness of detail, and (d) readability.

6. An anachronism is something out of its historical order, such as the striking of the clock in *Julius Caesar*. List several anachronisms from *Ivanhoe*.

7. Are Scott's characters like real people or are they in general stereotyped? Are there any exceptions? If so, comment on them.

8. The plot of *Ivanhoe* is loose and rambling but achieves unity at the end. Compare and contrast it with that of a novel like *A Tale of Two Cities,* in which every happening falls into place like a piece of jigsaw puzzle.

9. Mention one or more instances in which knowledge of a foreign language makes an immense difference in the outcome of certain events. (Chapter 5 and others)

10. Why is the character of Ulrica introduced? Does she add to the story or detract from it? Why? (Chapters 24-28)

11. The character of Rebecca is drawn from that of a real person. List her characteristics that are favorable in the eyes of the reader. Is she more lifelike than most of the other characters?

12. Many readers would prefer a different ending to *Ivanhoe*. In your opinion, would this have improved the book? Defend your answer. (Chapters 40-44)

13. In what ways did chivalry seek to glorify the Anglo-Saxon virtues still valued today? List them.

14. Give your evaluation of the archery contest as contrasted with the tournament. Does it add to or detract from the story? (Chapter 13)

15. Novels have heroes, heroines, and villains. *Ivanhoe* has more than one of each. Who are they? What are their characteristics as individuals?

16. According to history, Richard I forgave his brother John for attempting to seize the throne, saying that John had acted as a misguided child. He also pardoned the archer whose arrow gave him a fatal wound. Is Scott's portrayal of Richard in keeping with these facts?

17. The character of Isaac of York is a complex one, involving greed, race hatred, and parental affection. Discuss how Scott brings out each of these characteristics without underplaying the others.

18. The medieval clergy has received much criticism from Chaucer, Shakespeare, Scott, and other writers. From the characters of Prior Aymer, Friar Tuck, and Lucas Beaumanoir, Grand Master of the Temple, do you consider such criticism justified? Consider both sides of the question.

19. Do you consider the supposed death of Athelstane and his subsequent return to life an addition to the story or a flaw? Defend your answer.

SELECTED BIBLIOGRAPHY

WORKS BY SCOTT

Poetry

1802-03	Minstrelsy of the Scottish Border
1804	Sir Tristrem
1805	Lay of the Last Minstrel
1808	Marmion
1810	The Lady of the Lake
1811	The Vision of Don Roderick
1813	Rokeby The Bridal of Trierman
1815	The Lord of the Isles
1817	Harold the Dauntless

Novels

1814	Waverly
1815	Guy Mannering
1816	The Antiquary The Black Dwarf Old Mortality
1818	Rob Roy The Heart of Midlothian
1819	The Bride of Lammermoor The Legend of Montrose
1820	Ivanhoe The Monastery The Abbot
1821	Kenilworth
1822	The Pirate The Fortunes of Nigel

1823	Peveril of the Peak Quentin Durward
1824	St. Ronan's Well Redgauntlet
1825	The Betrothed The Talisman
1826	Woodstock
1827	Chronicles of the Canongate
1828	The Fair Maid of Perth
1829	Anne of Geierstein
1831	Count Robert of Paris Castle Dangerous

Miscellaneous

1808	Life and Works of John Dryden
1814	Life and Works of Jonathan Swift
1814-17	Border Antiquities of England and Scotland
1816	Paul's Letters to His Kinsfolk
1827	Life of Napoleon Buonaparte
1830	Letters on Demonology and Witchcraft

BIOGRAPHY AND CRITICISM

Allan, George. *Life of Sir Walter Scott*. Philadelphia: Crissy, Waldie & Co., 1835.

Beers, Henry A. *A History of English Romanticism in the Nineteenth Century*. New York: Henry Holt & Co., 1901.

Bos, Klaas. *Religious Creeds and Philosophies of Scott*. Amsterdam, 1932. Exchange dissertation of the University of Chicago.

Buchan, John. *Sir Walter Scott*. New York: Coward-McCann, Inc.; London: Cassell & Company, Ltd., 1932.

Canning, S. G. *History in Scott's Novels*. New York and Brooklyn: Ed. for America by A. Wessels Company; London: T. Fisher Unwin, 1907.

Crockett, W. S. *Scott Country,* 6th rev. ed. New York: The Macmillan Company; London: A. and C. Black, Ltd., 1930.

Davie, Donald. *The Heyday of Sir Walter Scott.* New York: Barnes & Noble, Inc.; London Routledge & Kegan Paul, Ltd., 1961.

Fiske, C. F. *Epic Suggestion in the Imagery of the Waverly Novels.* New Haven: Yale University Press; London: Oxford University Press, 1940.

Grierson, Sir Herbert [and others]. *Sir Walter Scott Lectures: 1940-1948.* Edinburgh: Edinburgh University Press, 1950.

Lockhart, John Gibson. *The Life of Sir Walter Scott.* New York: The Macmillan Company, 1914.

Muir, Edwin. *Scott and Scotland: The Predicament of the Scottish Writer.* London: George Routledge & Sons, Ltd., 1936; New York: Elliot Publishing Company, 1938.

Needler, George H. *Goethe and Scott.* London: Oxford University Press, 1950. New York: Oxford University Press, 1951.

Pearson, Hesketh. *Sir Walter Scott: His Life and Personality.* New York: Harper & Brothers, 1954.

Pope-Hennessy, Dame Una. *The Laird of Abbotsford: An Informal Presentation of Sir Walter Scott.* New York: G. P. Putnam's Sons, 1932.

Smock, George Edward. *Sir Walter Scott's Theory of the Novel: An Abstract of a Thesis.* Ithaca, New York, 1934.

NOTES

NOTES

NOTES

NOTES

NOTES

NOTES

NOTES